SONGBOOK SERIES REPERTOIRE
1

2ND EDITION

loan book #2

© Copyright 1998 The Frederick Harris Music Co., Limited
All Rights Reserved

ISBN 0-88797-623-9

Official Examination Repertoire of
The Royal Conservatory of Music
Grade 1

Répertoire officiel des examens
du Royal Conservatory of Music
Niveau 1

With the introduction of the 1998 Voice Syllabus, The Royal Conservatory of Music is pleased to present an expanded and revised edition of the *Songbook Series*, first published in 1991.

Building on the strengths of the first edition, the compilers of the series have retained many out-of-print materials for the convenience of students and teachers. Lengthening the books has allowed for the inclusion of more repertoire at each grade level.

Singers will welcome the variety and scope offered by the repertoire within these albums, which represents a broad spectrum of styles and musical periods, from Baroque to contemporary. Familiar Schubert Lieder and folk songs from many cultures are presented as well as delightful 20th-century songs of wit and humour and a sampling of Canadian works.

The compilers were sensitive to the need to choose repertoire suitable for young singers and singers with changing voices, in addition to keeping the adult student in mind. A small range chart at the top of each song will guide teachers in the selection of pieces suitable for their particular students' voices.

Songs in several languages other than English, French, and German are a unique feature of this collection. It is hoped that this multi-ethnic representation will encourage communication with the communities where those languages are spoken at home. Wherever possible, the original language as well as an English translation are underlaid with the music.

Metronome markings serve as suggestions for interpretation only. Where they appear in the source material, dynamics and articulation are given; otherwise, the compilers encourage a personal interpretation, especially for folk-song arrangements (in which it can be assumed that performance indications are editorial).

For details and requirements relating to The Royal Conservatory of Music voice examinations, teachers and students are advised to consult the current Voice Syllabus. While these albums serve as a ready resource for the preparation of examinations, their primary aim is to foster the love of singing and to support the development of the most precious instrument of all, the human voice.

Avec la présentation du nouveau Syllabus vocal de 1998, le Royal Conservatory of Music est heureux de présenter une édition revue et beaucoup plus élaborée de la *Songbook Series* de 1991.

Tout en considérant les points forts de la première édition, les spécialistes qui ont rassemblé les pièces formant cette collection ont gardé plusieurs morceaux hors catalogue afin d'accomoder professeurs et étudiants. De plus, en rallongeant le contenu des volumes, on a pu introduire davantage de répertoire propre à chaque niveau.

Les chanteurs accueilleront sûrement avec plaisir le choix varié et l'étendue du répertoire de ces albums. Ils pourront constater une vaste représentation de styles et d'épogues musicales partant du Baroque jusqu'à la musique contemporaine. Les Lieder de Schubert les plus familiers et les folklores provenant de différentes cultures ainsi que des charmantes mélodies du 20e siècle pleines de verve et d'humour avec en plus une bonne sélection de musique canadienne, font partie de cette collection.

On pourra noter aussi que les personnes en charge de ce project ont choisi avec soin des pièces appropriées aux jeunes chanteurs, ceux dont la voix change, en plus de penser aux étudiants adultes. La tessiture de chaque mélodie est indiquée au haut de la page afin de guider les professeurs dans leur choix. Des chansons autres que françaises, anglaises ou allemandes offrent un aspect unique de cette collection. Ceci a été voulu afin d'encourager une certaine communication au sein des communautés multi-ethniques, où ces langues sont parlées à la maison. Autant que possible, la langue originale ainsi qu'une traduction anglaise apparaissent avec la musique.

Les indications de métronome sont inscrites seulement à titre de suggestion pour l'interprétation. Les dynamiques et les phrasés sont donnés lorsqu'ils proviennent de la source originale autrement, nous encourageons une interprétation personelle, spécialement pour les arrangements folkloriques où ces indications sont plutôt éditoriales.

Pour plus de détails et une meilleure connaissance des exigences en rapport avec les examens de chant du Royal Conservatory of Music, nous conseillons aux étudiants de consulter le nouveau Syllabus. Il demeure que même si ces albums sont une ressource incomparable pour la préparation des examens, leur but premier est de susciter l'amour du chant et d'aider au développement du plus précieux des instruments, la voix humaine.

Table of Contents

4	Vive la canadienne/ My Canadian Girl	*French-Canadian folk song, arr. Hugh J. McLean*
6	Some Folks	*Stephen Collins Foster*
8	Jesous Ahatonhia	*16th-century French melody, arr. Healey Willan*
10	Skye Boat Song	*Highland rowing measure, arr. Malcom Lawson*
12	Mariann' s'en va-t-au moulin/ Marianne Went to the Mill	*French-Canadian folk song, arr. Claude Champagne*
14	Where Have You Been All the Day	*English folk song, arr. Adam Carse*
16	Ein Männlein steht/ There Stands a Little Man	*German folk song, arr. Ernest MacMillan*
17	Cicerenella	*Neapolitan melody, arr. Will Earhart*
20	The Carrion Crow	*English folk song, arr. Adam Carse*
23	Bobsledding	*Dean Blair*
26	Dragons	*Clifford Crawley*
29	Who Has Seen the Wind?	*Udo Kasemets*
30	The Wind	*Cecil Sharman*
32	Some Day	*David Ouchterlony*
34	Lullaby	*Nancy Telfer*
36	Little Leprechaun	*Clifford Crawley*
38	The Spider Hunter	*W.H. Anderson*
40	The Giraffe	*Clare Grundman*
43	La pomme et l'escargot/ The Apple and the Snail	*Darius Milhaud*

Some Folks

Stephen Collins Foster

Stephen Collins Foster
(1826 – 1864)

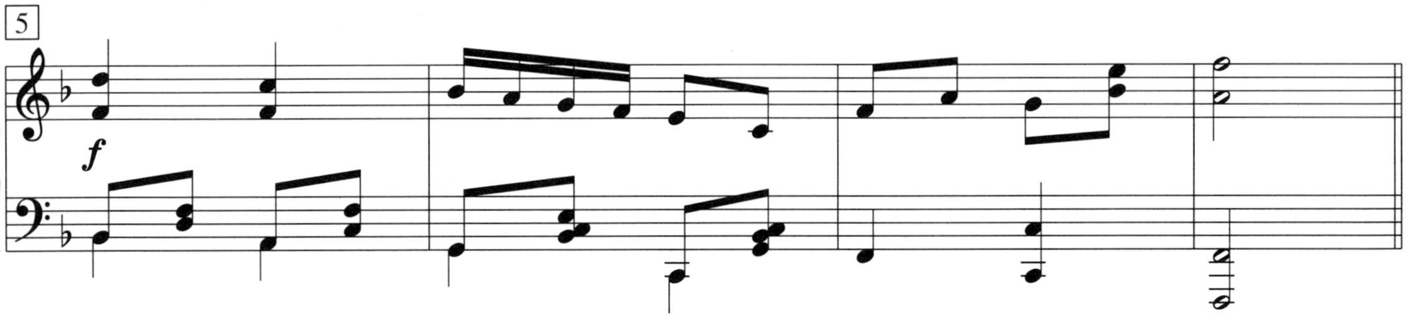

Moderato ♩ = 100 – 108

Jesous Ahatonhia

attr. Jean de Brébeuf
(1563 – 1649)
English words: Jesse Edgar Middleton

16th-century French melody
arr. Healey Willan

According to popular belief, this carol was written in 1642 by Jean de Brébeuf, a Jesuit missionary to the Huron people. The melody resembles the French folk song *Une jeune pucelle*. In the 1740s, Père de Villeneuve, a Jesuit priest in Lorette, Québec, transcribed the Huron text and tune, and Paul Picard, an Indian notary, made a French translation.
J.E. Middleton's English adaptation also appears in Healey Willan's pageant *Brébeuf* (1943).

Source: *Two Christmas Carols* (1927)

English words © copyright 1927 The Frederick Harris Music Co., Limited, Mississauga, Ontario, Canada.
Arrangement © copyright 1927 The Frederick Harris Music Co., Limited. Copyright assigned 1994 to Leslie Music Supply, Inc., Oakville, Ontario, Canada. Used by permission.

Skye Boat Song

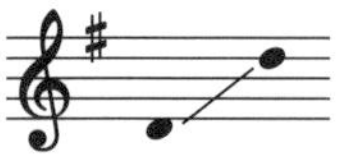

Harold Edwin Boulton
(1859 – 1935)

Highland rowing measure
arr. Malcom Lawson

Speed bonnie boat like a bird on the wing, onward the sailors cry; Carry the lad that's born to be king

After the defeat of the Jacobites at the Battle of Culloden on 16 April 1746, Prince Charles Edward Stuart spent five months in the highlands and islands of Scotland, on the run from British troops with a price of £30,000 on his head. In June 1746, he escaped to the Island of Skye with Flora Macdonald and a handful of loyal highlanders. The first four measures of this melody were taken down from the singing of Hebridean boatmen. The remainder were added by A.C. Macleod.

Source: *Songs of the North, Gathered from the Highlands and Lowlands of Scotland* (ed. A.C. Macleod and Harold Boulton, music arr. Malcolm Lawson)

© Copyright revived 1995 Cramer Music Ltd. Used by permission.

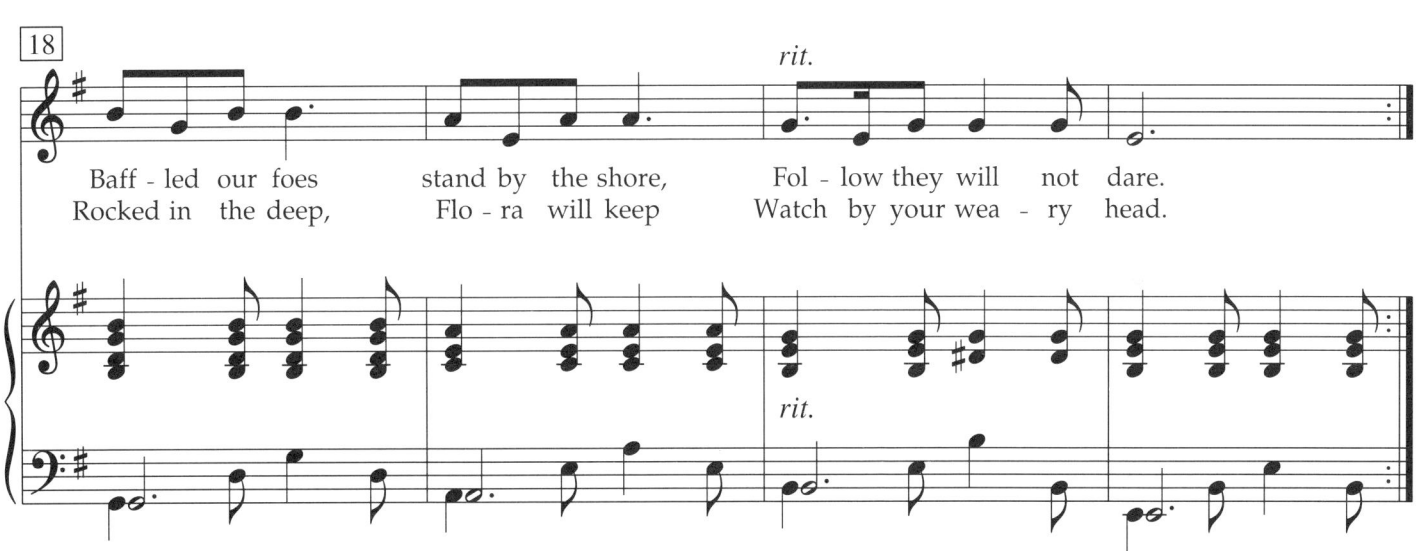

Mariann' s'en va-t-au moulin / Marianne Went to the Mill

Traditional French-Canadian
trans. Amy Bissett England

French-Canadian folk song
arr. Claude Champagne

1. Ma-ri-ann' s'en va-t-au mou-lin, Ma-ri-ann' s'en va-t-au mou-lin, C'est pour y fair' mou-dre son grain, c'est pour y fair' mou-dre son grain, À
1. Once Ma-ri-anne went to the mill, once Ma-ri-anne went to the mill With grain to grind and sack to fill, with grain to grind and sack to fill. She

(2.) dant que le mou-lin mar-chait, pen-dant que le mou-lin mar-chait, Le loup tout à l'en-tour rô-dait, le loup tout à l'en-tour rô-dait. Le
(2.) while the mil-ler ground her grain, then, while the mil-ler ground her grain A hun-gry wolf came down the lane, a hun-gry wolf came down the lane And

(3.) ri-ann' se mit à pleu-rer, Ma-ri-ann' se mit à pleu-rer, Cent é-cus d'or lui a don-né, cent é-cus d'or lui a don-né, Pour
(3.) when the mil-ler heard her cry, and when the mil-ler heard her cry, He gave her gold-en coins to buy, he gave her gold-en coins to buy An-

Arrangement and English words © copyright 1959 The Frederick Harris Music Co., Limited. Copyright assigned 1991 to Claude Champagne. Reprinted by permission of the estate of Claude Champagne.

Where Have You Been All the Day?

Traditional English

English folk song
arr. Adam Carse

Source: *Four Old Nursery Rhymes*, no. 3
Arrangement © copyright 1928 Stainer & Bell Limited, London, England. Used by permission.

Ein Männlein steht / There Stands a Little Man

Traditional German
trans. Constance Bache

German folk song
arr. Ernest MacMillan

Andante ♩ = 84 – 92

1. Ein Männ-lein steht im Wal-de ganz still und stumm; es hat von lau-ter Pur-pur ein Mänt-lein um.
  Sagt, wer mag das Männ-lein sein, das da steht im Wald al-lein mit dem pur-pur-ro-ten
1. *There stands a lit-tle man in the wood a-lone. He wears a lit-tle man-tle of vel-vet brown.*
  Say who can the man-kin be, Stand-ing there be-neath the tree, With his lit-tle man-tle of

(2.) Männ-lein steht im Wal-de auf ei-nem Bein und hat auf sei-nem Ko-pfe schwartz käpp-lein klein.
  Sagt, wer mag das Männ-lein sein, das da steht auf ei-nem Bein mit dem klei-nen schwar-zen
(2.) *hair is all of gold, and his cheeks are red. He wears a lit-tle black cap up-on his head.*
  Say who can the man-kin be, Stand-ing there so si-lent-ly, With his lit-tle black cap up-

Source: Gretel sings this song in act 2, scene 1 of *Hänsel und Gretel*, an opera by Engelbert Humperdinck (1854–1921).
The arrangement used here is from *A Canadian Song Book* (ed. Ernest MacMillan).
Arrangement © copyright 1929 J.M. Dent & Sons. Used by permission of the estate of Sir Ernest MacMillan.

Cicerenella

Traditional Neapolitan
trans. Will Earhart

Neapolitan melody
arr. Will Earhart

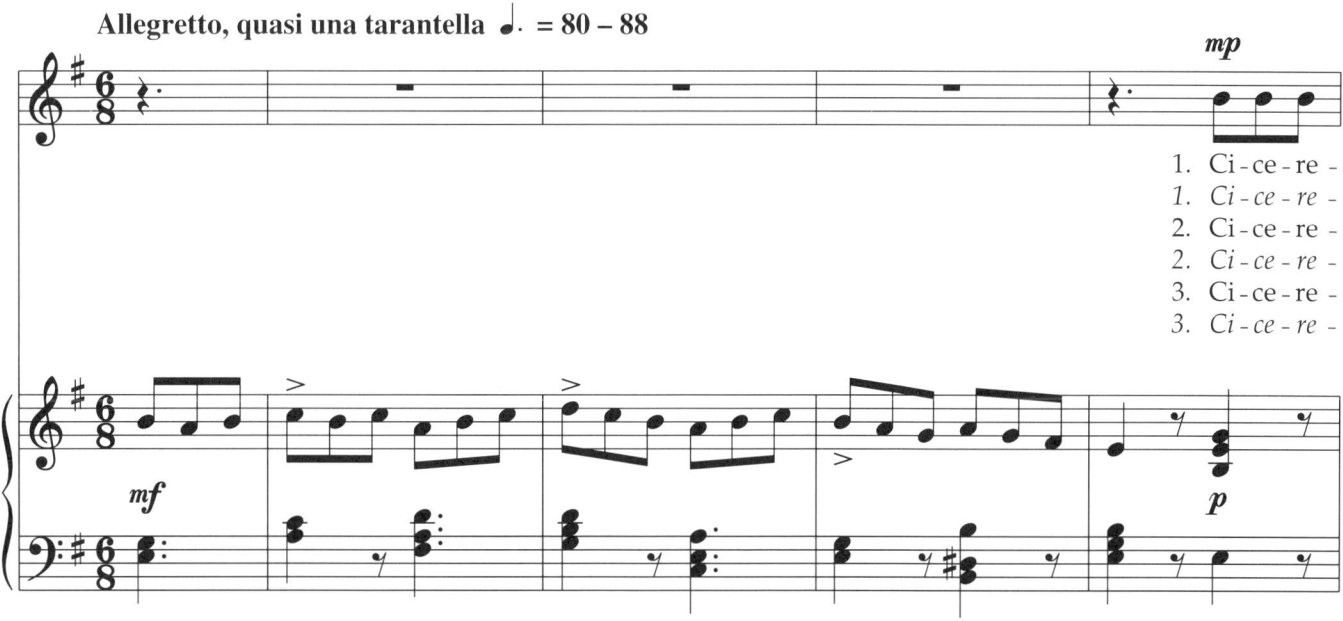

Source: *Pathways of Song*, vol. 4 (ed. and trans. Frank La Forge and Will Earhart)
© Copyright 1938 M. Witmark & Sons, New York. Used by permission of Warner/Chappell Music Canada Ltd.

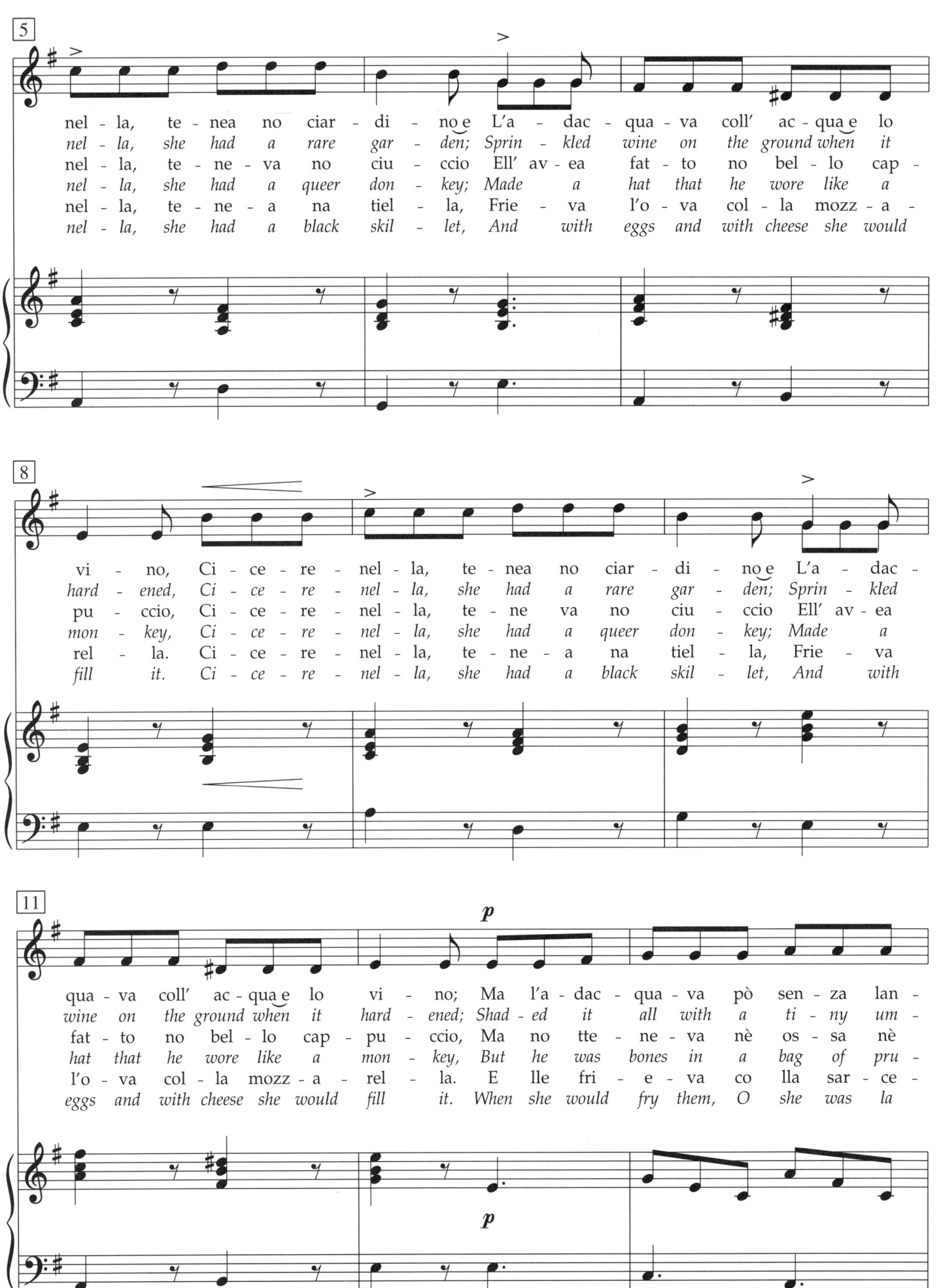

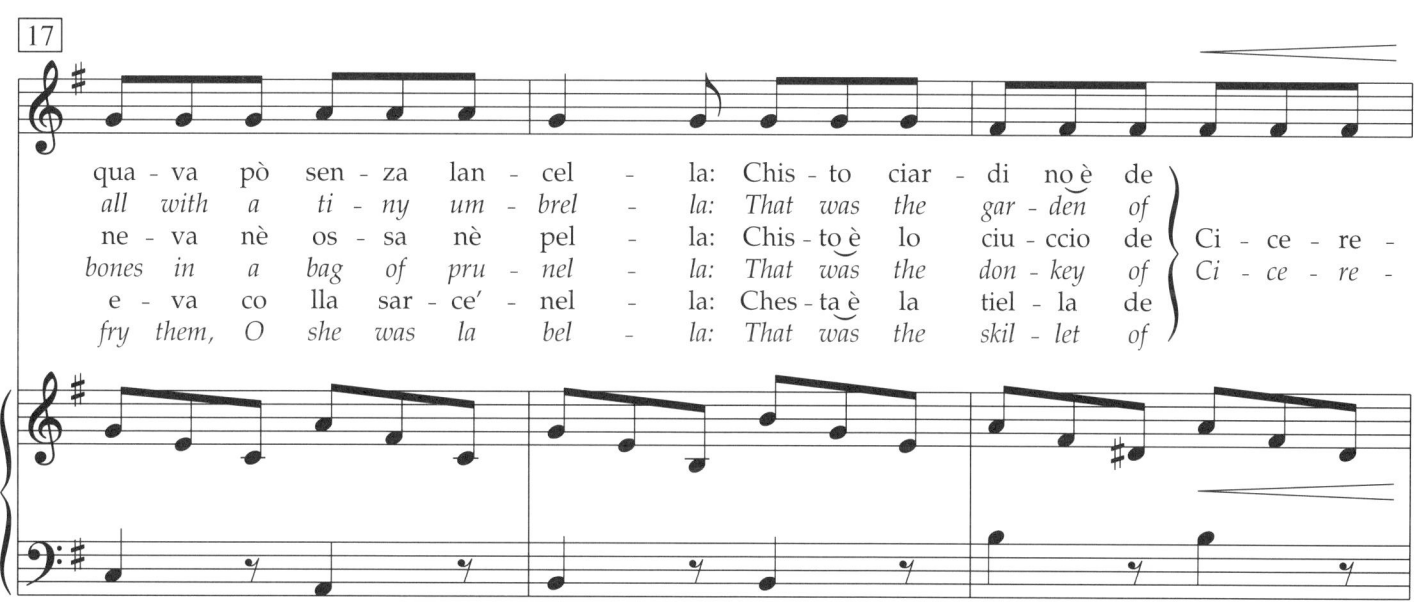

The Carrion Crow

Traditional English

English folk song
arr. Adam Carse

Allegretto ♩ = 80 – 88

1. A carrion crow sat on an oak, Derry, derry, derry,
(2.) wife! bring me my old bent bow,
(3.) tailor shot and miss'd his mark,

dee-co; A carrion crow sat on an oak, That
O wife! bring me my old bent bow, And
The tailor shot and miss'd his mark,

Watching a tailor shape his cloak, Heigh ho, the carrion crow,
I may shoot yon carrion crow,
shot his own sow through the heart,

The carrion crow *(corras corone)*, known in Scotland as a *corbie,* is a common species of crow that feeds on small animals and carrion. It is a little smaller than a raven and has black plumage.

Source: *Four Old Nursery Rhymes,* no. 4

Arrangement © copyright 1928 Stainer & Bell, Limited, London, England. Used by permission.

Bobsledding

Dean Blair

Dean Blair
(1932 –)

Marcato ♩ = 104 – 112

1. When the snow is fall-ing down
2. Haul the old sled up the hill.
3. On the sled we're flash-ing by

And the drifts are on the ground, then you know it's bob-sled time.
Through the woods and past the mill. Find the old road down the slope.
Down the run at speeds so high. Hold on tight and don't let go.

I can hard-ly wait. Hope I'm not too late.
Take a tri-al run. It will be great fun.
Rac-ing down the hill. Let's not have a spill.

Source: *Six Playful Songs*, no. 6

© Copyright 1991 Alberta Keys Music Publishing Co. Ltd. Used by permission.

Dragons

Clifford Crawley

Clifford Crawley
(1929 –)

Source: *Creatures Great and Small*, set 1
© Copyright 1986 Leslie Music Supply Inc., Oakville, Ontario, Canada. Used by permission.

Who Has Seen the Wind?

Christina Georgina Rossetti
(1830 – 1894)

Udo Kasemets
(1919 –   )

Source: *Five Songs for Children*, no. 5

© Copyright 1964 BMI Canada Limited, Toronto, Canada. Used by permission of Berandol Music Limited.

The Wind

Enid Blyton
(1897 – 1968)

Cecil Sharman
(–1973)

Source: *Songs of Autumn*

© Copyright 1935 Banks & Son (Music) Ltd. Copyright transferred 1972 to Banks Music Publications. Used by permission.

10
p
cresc. e poco accel.
They're off in a flur-ry, And whis-per and scur-ry, For
p
cresc. e poco accel.
13
f
oh, the wind's in such a ter - ri - ble hur - ry.
f
15
a tempo
pp
mf
Woo
Woo
a tempo
pp
mf
p

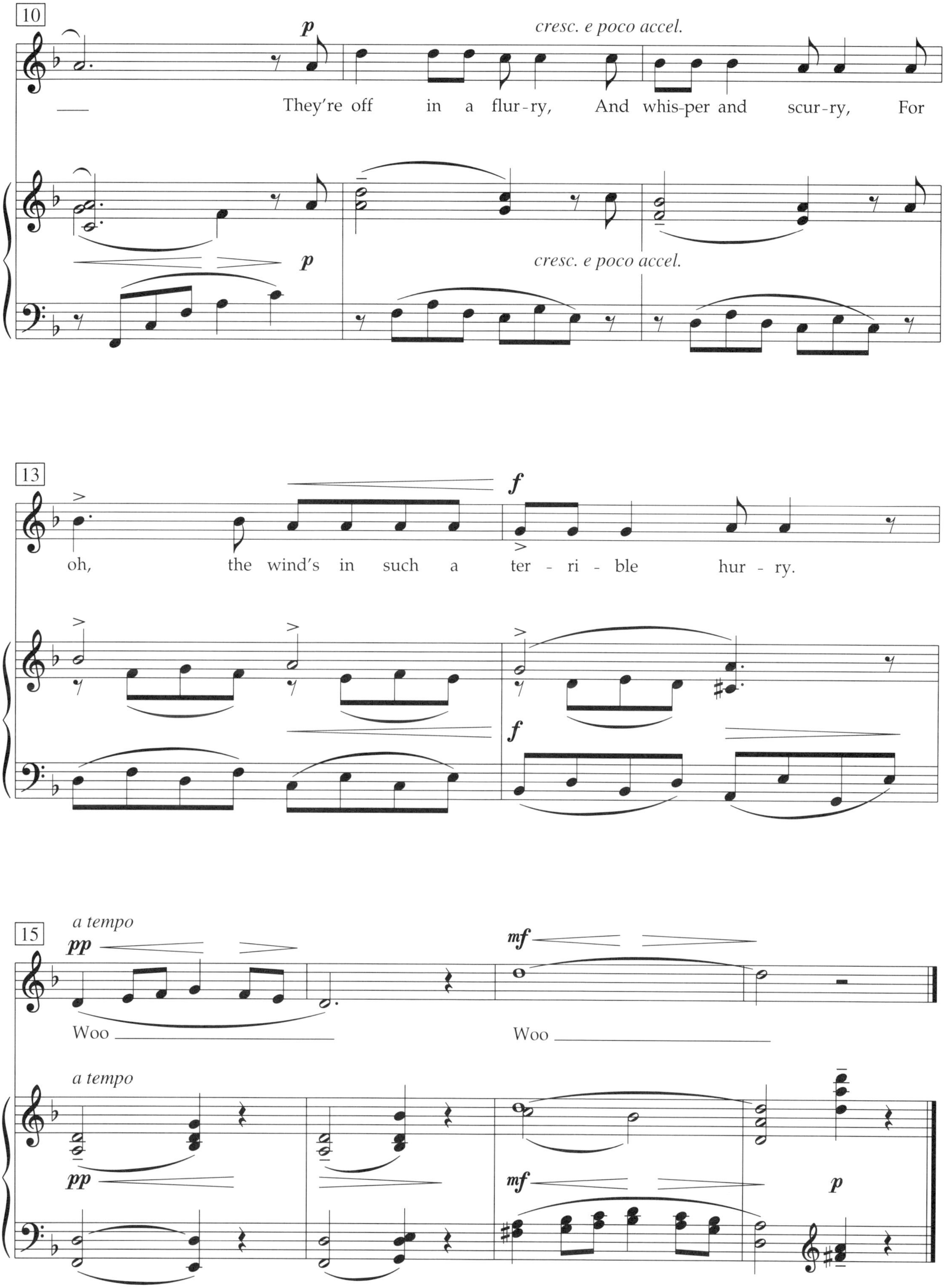

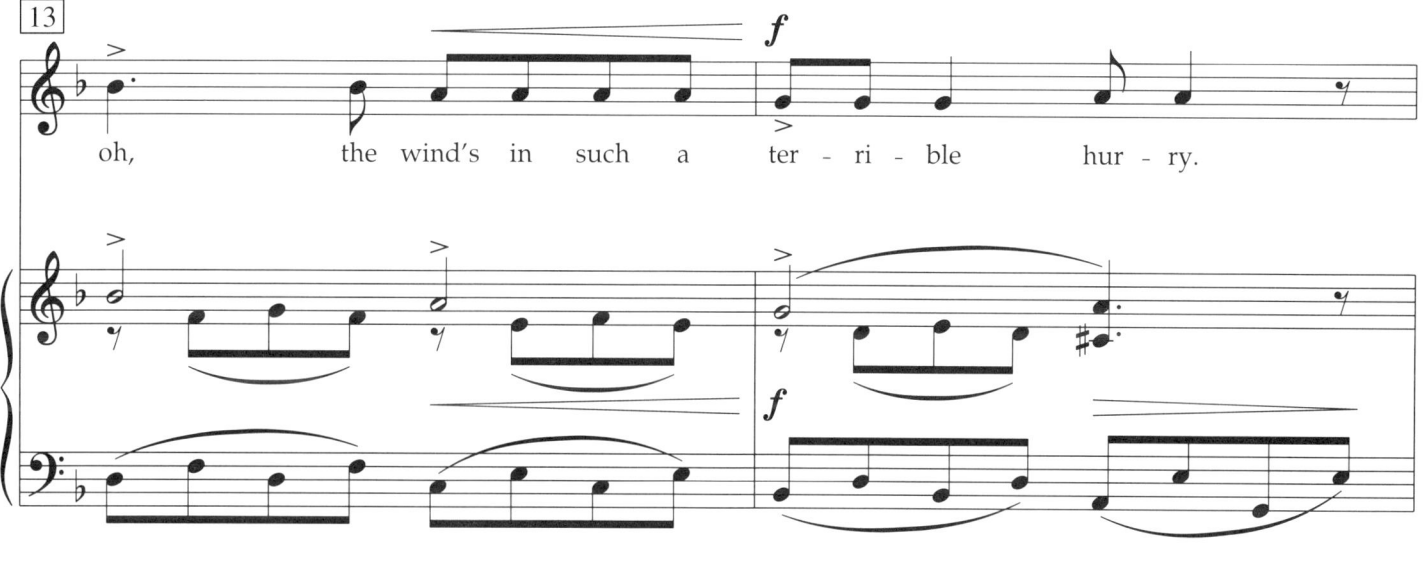

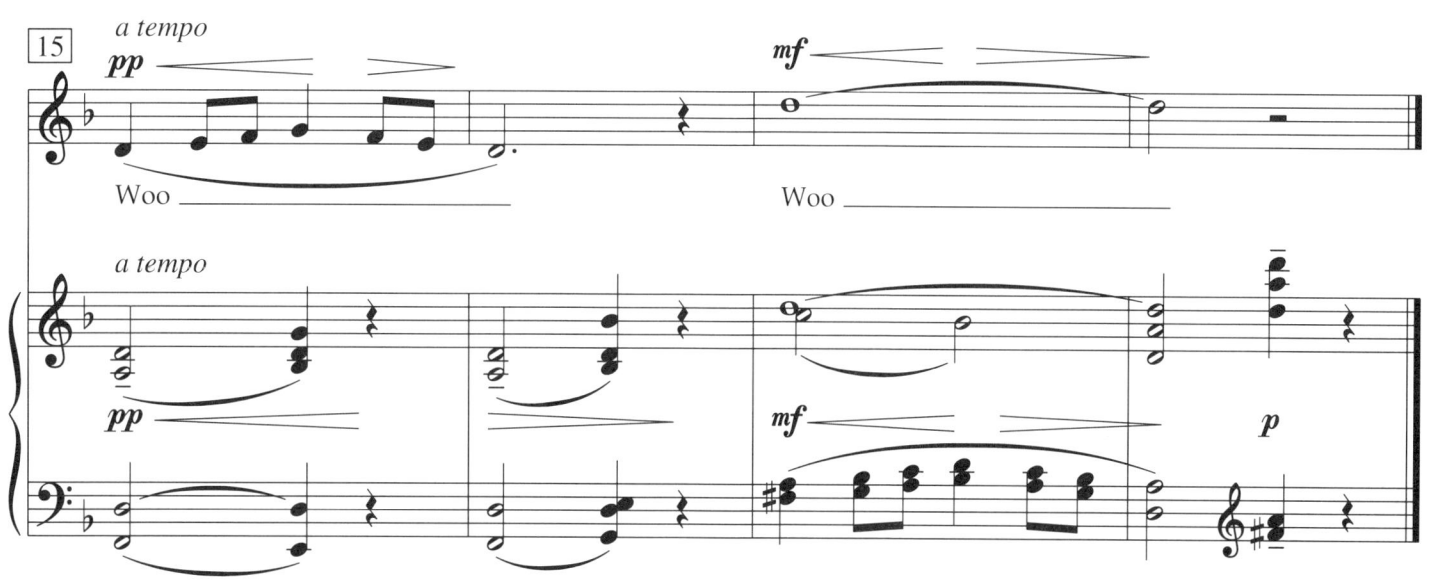

Some Day

David Ouchterlony

David Ouchterlony
(1914 – 1987)

Cheerfully / Gaiement ♩ = 112 – 120

1. Some day, when I am big and older, eight or nine, or even ten. Some day, I think I'll be a soldier, marching down the street and then back again, or perhaps a fireman racing by or a po-
2. Some day, you may be riding in a bus, or travelling in a train. Some day, you may be wond'ring who's the brave and clever pilot of your aeroplane, and it may be driver, engineer or

Source: *Three Songs for Very Young People*

© Copyright 1982 Leslie Music Supply Inc., Oakville, Ontario, Canada. Used by permission.

Lullaby

Nancy Telfer

Nancy Telfer
(1950 –)

© Copyright 1987 Leslie Music Supply Inc., Oakville, Ontario, Canada. Used by permission.

Little Leprechaun

Clifford Crawley

Clifford Crawley
(1929 –)

Vivace ♩ = 126 – 138

p sempre leggiero

Lit-tle, lit-tle, lit-tle, lit-tle Lep-re-chaun, Don't sit there look-ing all for-lorn, Lit-tle, lit-tle, lit-tle, lit-tle Lep-re-chaun,

1. Come and play with me! We'll play games, and I'll
2. Come and dance with me! Please don't wor-ry be-
3. Come and sing with me! You sing high notes and

© Copyright 1988 Leslie Music Supply Inc., Oakville, Ontario, Canada. Used by permission.

The Spider Hunter
to David and Paul

Lawrence Phillips

W. H. Anderson
(1882 – 1955)

I saw a fun-ny gob-lin with hair up-on his face, A-

climb-ing up a lad-der in a cur-tain lace. His nose was long and crook-ed, his

teeth were sharp and clean. He had hooks up-on his toe-nails and his

Source: *The Western Song Books*, book 1 (composed and arranged by W. H. Anderson)
© Copyright 1938 Western Music Company, Ltd., Vancouver and Winnipeg, Canada. Used by permission of Leslie Music Supply, Oakville, Ontario, Canada.

The Giraffe

Clare Grundman

Clare Grundman
(1913 –)

Source: *Zoo Illogical*, no. 4
© Copyright 1974 Boosey & Hawkes, Inc. Used by permission.

La pomme et l'escargot / The Apple and the Snail
Op. 67, No. 1

Charles Vildrac
(1882 – 1971)
trans. Hugh J. McLean

Darius Milhaud
(1892 – 1974)

Source: *Cinq chansons de Charles Vildrac*, op. 67 (1937)
Music and French words © copyright Editions Salabert. Used by permission.
English translation © copyright 1991 The Frederick Harris Music Co., Limited, Mississauga, Ontario, Canada.